T0105791

UNCONDITIONAL
Forbidden Love

VICKI CASE

BALBOA.
PRESS
A DIVISION OF HAY HOUSE

Balboa Press books may be ordered through booksellers or by contacting:

Balboa Press
A Division of Hay House
1663 Liberty Drive
Bloomington, IN 47403
www.balboapress.com.au
1-(877) 407-4847

ISBN: 978-1-4525-0407-0 (sc)
ISBN: 978-1-4525-0408-7 (e)

Printed in the United States of America

Balboa Press rev. date: 02/16/2012

DEDICATION

This book is dedicated to the only man
I have ever really loved, my soul mate,
my Eros and my Adonis; all rolled into one.

Some people live their life;
Yet fail to leave an impression;
Others shoot into our lives;
Etching their mark eternally on our souls.

You have touched my life; my soul;
Like no other person before you;
I want to bear my soul;
Open up my inner most secrets; to you.

The inner turmoil is unrelenting;
The head & heart struggle; difficult;
Life is so short; yet can last for decades;
Lifetimes passing in a flash.

Priceless is knowing what it is you want;
Courage, having the strength to pursue it;
Stupidity, the time we waste; deciding;
Tolerance; the patience I have shown to date.

Follow your heart; chase your dreams;
We may only have tonight;
Only God knows what awaits us;

Even the toughest bull can be spooked by a storm;
Acknowledge, what it is you've been offered;
Tell me how you feel; what it is you want;
No more regrets; make time for us.

I love you my handsome love;
I love you with all my heart;
I think about you every waking moment;
My dreams filled with you every night.

You have touched my heart;
Like no other before you;
In places I never knew existed;
Your mark forever etched therein.

Before fate brought us together;
I was wondering aimlessly; lost in a fog;
A horse without a spirit;
A rod without a reel.

I have never felt so scared; so vulnerable;
As I do about you; 'The Forbidden Fruit';
I could not once find words to say;
How it was I felt, until now, until you.

You are so incredibly handsome;
So sexy, so desirable;
You're beautiful eyes; your warm smile;
They say so much, yet divulge so little.

My eyes can't wait to see you again;
My arms long to embrace you;
My mouth to taste you;
My body to feel you.

My love for you is real & strong;
I will not diminish these feelings;
Although they appear to frighten you;
Spooking you to retreat, back away;
You mean the world to me;
I need & want you in my life;
You deserve to be loved;
And know that you are loved.

You are a jewel that enriches my life;
The sun that lights my way;
The moonlight that guides me to dream;
The breath that gives me life;
The spirit that inspires me;
The strength that gives me courage;
The reason that gives me hope;
My heart's twin & soul mate.

You are a rarity; inspired by the Gods;
So charming & chivalrous;
Impressively beautiful & sweet;
Conspicuously brilliant;
Incredibly sexy & very desirable;
Gentle, caring & passionate;
'The Forbidden Fruit';
Every woman's dream come true.

I don't know how else to tell you;
That I love you handsome;
To let you know my heart is yours;
To show you how much I care.

I thought I'd loved only twice before;
That was until I met you;
Then I came to realise;
I'd never really loved at all.

I think about you night & day;
My dreams of you so vivid;
My desire for you insatiable;
My love for you undisputed.

I've never done for another;
The things I've said & done for you;
The poems, those photos; the written declarations;
All for you & straight from my heart.

You have challenged & tested my love;
On more than one occasion;
Yet I've never yielded an inch;
What does that tell you about me?

That my love for you is real?
That I love you Handsome?
And that I always will?

Fate brought us together;
That winter of '01;
Little did I know then;
Thoughts of you would consume me.

I'm just another set of eyes;
In a sea of eyes;
I'm just another person;
A body in a crowd.

He doesn't know that I exist;
Hasn't got a clue I care;
Doesn't know I want him;
My love for him unknown.

What started as a desire;
Grew into love; so easily;
Sometimes we're not aware;
What's standing right in front of us.

God he is so handsome;
Sculptured by the Gods;
So beautifully exquisite;
The mould thereafter broken.

My thoughts are filled with him;
My dreams bring him to life;
How I yearn to utter the words;
I love you.

You are so handsome;
You've captured my heart;
I'm captivated;
Attracted by your charm.

You are so beautiful;
You dominate my thoughts;
I'm inspired;
Filled with awe & wonder.

You are so amazing;
Nightly stealing my dreams;
A state of spiritual blessedness;
Til' the alarm shatters the bliss.

You are so incredible;
I've surrendered you my soul;
I look at you;
There is no one else I see.

I pray you will never tire;
Don't get sick of hearing;
Never request they cease;
My expressions of love for you.

I love you Handsome;
You are my heart, my soul, my treasure;
How many ways can I tell you?
How many stars grace the night sky?

Your name is engraved on my heart;
Embedded in my thoughts;
Tattooed on my soul; and
The star of my nightly dreams.

Emery will not erase the etching;
Denial will not make it not so;
Water will not wash away the ink;
Nor; not sleeping the answer.

Your love may all be taken;
Your heart may not be free;
But if you shall ever need me;
You know that I'll be there.

I'll never stop loving you Handsome;
I know because I've tried;
You are my today, my tomorrow and my forever;
You are a truly amazing guy.

Throughout life we meet many people;
Many never really touch us;
Just passerby's on life's road;
Then I met you.

You are so beautiful & handsome;
So special, so charming;
You can have any woman you want;
Anyone; at the click of your fingers.

Love is measured by the heart;
If you love someone; then tell them;
I am in love with you;
I will always love you Handsome.

I'm scared that you will tire; though
Bore of my daily adulations;
Grow weary of my adoration;
Dread those three words; I love you.

Whilst there's blood in my veins;
Breath fills my lungs;
My hands & voice can express;
I will tell you of my love for you.

So many thoughts & feelings;
Where do I begin?
I'll start with my heart;
And what I feel therein.

You have captured my heart;
That first moment I saw you;
My soul was soon to follow;
But you know this to be true.

I look into your green eyes;
It's so hard to turn away;
Then there's that beautiful smile;
It takes my breath away.

So many faces in a crowd;
Yet yours is all I can see;
If only you could understand;
What you do to me.

I love you for who you are;
The whole package that is you;
You have the key to my heart;
But this you already knew.

I love you with all my being;
More than words can say;
I will wait for all eternity;
For a chance that may.

You've bought out the best in me;
I'll never be the same;
Turn around & see whose chasing;
You will know my name.

I may not be the most gorgeous;
I may not stop a crowd;
But no one could love you more;
If only I were allowed.

I may only be of country blood;
I may not look great in a dress;
My bodies not the most amazing;
But I will always love you the best.

You could search the whole world over;
But I know you'll never find;
No matter how hard you look;
A love that's quite like mine.

You are the love of my life;
You personify beauty in every way;
You are my God of love & lust;
So much I want to say.

Your grandiose beauty;
Makes me tremble so;
I get lost in your aura;
But this you already know.

Your emanating radiance;
Makes my heart race;
You are my inspiration;
No one will ever replace.

I am never alone;
You are always in my thoughts;
Oh my handsome Eros;
This just cannot be bought.

You easily put me in heaven;
When I hear your voice;
Read your words; see your face;
I just want to rejoice.

You are a prominent figure;
You must commend my persistence;
I love & need you in my life;
Your essence validates my existence.

I love you Handsome;
This you know to be so;
But above all else;
This I want you to know.

I love you more than you know;
I'd give you the world if I could;
I'd go through hell for a kiss;
If only you would.

You matter My Love;
You are truly amazing;
Let no one tell you otherwise;
Turn around; I'll be there gazing.

There's a true beauty to a poem;
Written by hand, from your heart;
If I'd never met you; however
I wouldn't know where to start.

My heart aches when you're not near
It's like my throat has been cut;
I never stop thinking about you;
Christ, I must be a nut.

I see you everywhere;
I just want you;
You stir my heart like no other;
This you already know to be true.

Life is full of such beauty; but
Love is a moment that lasts forever;
There is only one happiness in life;
To love & to be loved.

Another time; another place
Will we ever really know?
Brief though it was, it was;
Beautiful, special & memorable.

We met in the winter of '01;
Our lives both at a crossroads;
My life was my own;
Yours belonged to another.

Destiny bought us together;
Fate predetermined the outcome;
Nothing lasts forever, or so they say;
But it was worth the ride.

You are the love of my life;
I've never known such exhilarating love;
We never go to where I'd like;
But I consider myself very fortunate.

Some people never find love;
Their true love & soul mate;
Forever chasing that pot of gold;
Most end up bitter & confused.

You came into my life & made a difference;
You stole my heart, touched my soul & became my dreams;
You've touched me like no other;
You etched your name forever on my heart.

I never knew how exciting love could be;
The explosion of passion in my heart;
New Year's fireworks; it's never abated;
You gave an old dog a second chance.

You enriched my spirit & my soul;
My once dull & uneventful dreams now;
Vivid & passionate cinema extravaganzas;
I've never known such desire; such love.

Words of love cascade into my thoughts;
A tsunami of words flood my head;
Expression & poetic license, now mine;
Our love forever captured in ink.

Nothing lasts forever; it is said
You were not there for the taking;
Alas, belonging to another;
Oh, to walk in her shoes for a day.

If I'd never met you;
I'd never have known true love;
How to feel, to want, to desire;
I'm glad for the experience with you.

My heart has left its home;
Gone from the chest that once held it;
Taking up residence elsewhere;
Now residing in the pit of my stomach.

My heart's vowed never to return;
Return to where it was broken;
A mere shell of its former self;
Never gone though; the love it has for you.

I could sit & lament what was;
Or, what could have been;
To scoff, grow angry; but
Our paths were chosen for us.

They say; if you love something, let it go;
I pray that one day you seek me out;
Rediscover our love in each other's arms;
Two hearts becoming one.

I've discovered a feeling;
A feeling I can't explain;
Like the look of a rose; or
The smell that comes with rain.

If I know what love is;
It's all because of you;
The first time you looked at me;
My heart knew it was true.

I gave you all my love & trust;
Since the first day we met;
It was given to you to keep;
Nothing more you have to get.

When I tell you 'I love you';
I want to make sure you know;
Not to hear it back;
So you remember it; make you glow.

I may not see you often;
Or get to hold you at night;
But deep inside my heart;
I know what I feel is right.

I love you so much it scares me;
No matter what; I'll always love you;
If for one moment, you could be me;
You'd know how much this I say is true.

I've never once lied to you;
Everything straight from my heart;
All my words & feelings true;
This is where I had to start.

When I tell you 'I love you';
I do, I really & truly do;
No three words mean more;
& I've said them all to you.

When I say you are Handsome;
You are, please believe me;
No one comes close to you;
Not a sole that I can see.

When I tell you I love those eyes;
Those eyes that captivate me;
I'm hypnotised by them;
Look into mine and see.

Your voice is so beautiful;
I love listening to you;
I could listen to you forever;
Believe what I say, it's true.

You have an internal beauty;
It permeates from within;
Your soft & gentle side;
Hey, it's not a sin.

Then there's that magical aura;
That makes your presence felt;
You are so beautiful & special;
Me, I just melt.

How do I explain my love to you?
What a difference you make in my life?
I don't have to tell you 'I love you';
For you know that it is true.

You call my attraction 'lust';
A sinful, sensuous appetite;
A desire to satisfy a bodily need;
A feeling that fades with time.

I call my feelings 'love';
My affection for you deep & intense;
Love isn't what I say;
Love is what I do.

I've loved you from the day I met you;
Not a day goes by that I don't think of you;
I don't know how to say it better;
Then to write it down in ink.

Words alone can't express my feelings;
How strong my love is burning;
God blessed me with you in my life;
I will never ask for anything more.

Behind those beautiful eyes;
Lies the most beautiful soul;
So warm & so passionate;
But not everyone knows.

Your arms are my favourite place;
When you take me in your arms;
I forget everything in your embrace;
My world pauses its spin.

I love the way you kiss me;
Your lips so soft & gentle;
When your lips touch mine;
I feel the sweetness of heaven.

I love it when you say my name;
You say it & I just melt;
I love the way you look at me;
Your eyes so beautiful & green.

I love the way you touch me;
The feel of your gentle hands on me;
Your touch like nothing I've ever known;
Sending my body into orgasm heaven.

I love the warmth of your breath;
The aura of your natural fragrance;
I love looking into your eyes; and
Telling you how I feel about you.

You touch my body; you touch my mind;
I love laying my head on your chest;
I love exploring you with my hungry fingertips;
Our private moments; beautiful & special.

There is magic in your beautiful eyes;
You exemplify male pulchritude; and
With your physical comeliness;
You stand out from the crowd.

You are my hearts candle;
Which burns ever so bright;
When I am with you;
I pray the moment will never end.

Lust is when the mind desires;
What the heart admires;
Love is when the mind admires;
What the heart desires.

My mind knows what is right;
My heart knows what it wants;
Why am I so afraid to lose you?
When you belong to another.

Although we'll never be together;
You will forever be in my heart;
I hope one day you realise;
The love that I have for you.

I want to lose myself in your arms;
The amazing arms of an Angel;
You are the brightest star in my sky;
You are the torch that lit my fire.

You are imposing to look at;
Even the sun is jealous;
Of the way that you shine;
My love for you forever & always.

I am forever changed today;
Changed by who you are;
What you mean to me; and
The light you helped me see.

Tell me you read all my poems;
My declarations of love to you;
I very much need you to believe;
Everything I've ever said is true.

Words alone can't tell you;
Just how much I love you;
How you've touched my heart & soul;
What else could I possibly do?

You don't know what you do to me;
The way loving you makes me feel;
The life you've given back this soul;
My feelings for you are very real.

You are the wind beneath my wings;
That keeps me soaring high;
Whenever I'm in your presence;
I feel like I could fly.

You are the spark that relit my fire;
The fuel that makes me burn bright;
I only have to think of you;
& I glow brightly, even at night.

One of the worst things in life;
Is to miss the opportunity;
To tell someone how you feel;
The love that's in your heart.

So how can I tell you?
How much I truly love you?
In words I haven't already said:
Or ways I haven't already shown.

True love is knowing without a doubt;
Leaving no words left unsaid;
I love you means a lot;
I said it & I mean it.

I want to tell you today;
The difference you make in my life;
I know that you are my Angel;
You are the sun that makes me shine.

You are more valuable than gold;
You are living within my soul;
The most precious moment for me;
When you kiss me without control.

Your kiss on my lips gives me wings;
Your touch makes me sing;
You don't know how much I love you;
Forever you'll be the half that makes me whole.

Reams of paper written;
Heaven only knows how many pens;
To pour out my heart to you;
I've lost count of the Amen's.

Can you possibly conceive?
The love it takes to compose;
The multitude of poems;
I believe I deserve a rose.

Endless hours alone;
Only you on my mind;
Words & thoughts cascading;
Yet another line I must find.

Despite my valiant efforts;
I still don't have a clue;
What it is you think & feel;
A voice that has no hue.

Just once I'd wish you'd tell me;
What it is that's in your head;
Feelings you may have for me;
That would be a great start.

I love you too much, so much;
It wasn't by design;
This poem is for you;
Oh sweet love of mine.

I sense you feel awkward;
Each time I say 'I love you';
You've made me believe in love again;
I've found my love was true.

I write to you each day;
Even if I have nothing to say;
Because my love for you grows;
More & more each day.

There is something special about you;
That has captured my very soul;
I see beauty in you in many ways;
When I'm around you I lose control.

Your smile couldn't be more perfect;
I'd do anything to see you smile;
Your smile is to see the divine;
It always leaves me beguiled.

To look into your beautiful eyes;
Is to gaze into the sky;
Its stars; all so beautiful;
& the heavens inside; so high.

If you love someone;
Be brave enough to say;
'I love you Handsome';
More & more each day!

I feel I should say something complex;
Something long & drawn out;
To tell you how I feel about you;
That will leave you in no doubt.

But all I have to say is simple;
"I LOVE YOU';
My heart was lost forever;
The instant I saw you smile; it's true.

You made me fall in love with you;
If I never live to see another day;
Will you know 'I love you'?
If I never, ever say.

Heaven sent me an Angel to love;
And that Angel was you;
Love comes as easily as breathing;
Loving you; so very easy to do.

So when you look up at the stars;
I know you see the same thing I see;
But what I really want to know is;
When you look up; do you think of me?

'I love you Sweetness';
I just can't tell you enough;
I worry however; I tell you too much;
My love; please don't ever rebuff.

You are a truly amazing guy;
Each day 'I love you' more;
Please never doubt my love;
You are the one I truly adore.

My heart almost stopped once;
The day I told you 'I love you';
You never, ever leave my mind;
Not for a moment, that's true.

Love is the greatest power;
Love is a treasure;
I'm madly in love with you;
My love too vast to measure.

I've never looked upon such beauty;
You are like a fine wine;
Aged to perfection;
Our bodies I want to entwine.

You've turned my life around;
I've told you things;
I've never shared with another;
You've literally given me wings.

You've given me back so much;
Yet you don't have a clue;
The changes you're responsible for;
Oh, it is so very true.

When I say 'I love you';
I don't expect "I love you too';
I just want to see you smile;
& believe that I do love you.

Love is expressed in many ways;
True love expressed in one;
I need you to know what I feel;
I pray it's not overdone.

I know 'I love you';
I can't stop thinking about you;
I pray from time to time;
I might cross your mind too.

You've left your mark on my heart;
That will stand the test of time;
I try to tell you of my feelings;
Daily, in words that rhyme.

I very much need you to know;
No matter whatever & wherever;
Days will come & go;
But my love for you will be forever.

I try to write lyrical poems;
Words I've put together; that rhyme;
To express all that's in my heart;
But "I love you' says it all, every time.

I love you so deeply;
I love you so much;
I love the sound of your voice;
And the way that you touch.

I love your warm smile;
Your kind thoughtful ways;
& the joy you bring to my life;
Each & everyday.

I love you today;
As I have from the start;
& I'll love you forever;
With all of my heart.

No one will ever mean to me;
As much as what you do;
No matter what the ending;
My life began with you.

Roses are red;
Violets are blue;
Love never crossed my mind;
Until the day I met you.

Stocks are orange;
Chrysanthemums can be lime;
I very much need to tell you;
Just what's on my mind.

Hydrangeas are variegated;
Echinacea are green;
Just like your beautiful eyes;
Gorgeous & pristine.

Daffodils are yellow;
Lilies' are white;
My dreams of you;
Vivid & bright.

Hibiscuses are many colours;
Calla Lilies are wine;
How I very much want;
Our bodies to entwine.

Carnations are multi-coloured;
Silver thistles are grey;
Forever & a day;
In love with you I'll stay.

Iris's are cream;
Pansies come in colours galore;
My love for you;
To vast to ignore.

Lavender is purple;
Orchids are peach pink;
It worries me deeply;
Just what you think.

Always in my heart;
Always deep within my soul;
I am under your spell;
I've lost all self-control.

Thoughts of you make me tremble;
A fire rages deep inside my heart;
Time with you passes too quickly;
I dread it when you have to depart.

I still taste your kiss on my lips;
Alone, I hunger for those kisses tonight;
How I long to see you again soon;
Being with you is a sheer delight.

I love your beautiful gentle hands;
The space between your fingers;
Created for mine to fill;
Your touch on my body; still lingers.

You have left a fire burning;
A fire only you can put out;
I long to return to your open arms;
My love for you; please never doubt.

The greatest thing we ever learn;
Is to love, & in return be loved;
How do I tell you, my Darling?
Thou art a man greatly beloved.

My thoughts of you are most intense;
2am in the morning; the time;
When words & thoughts cascade;
All along; till the next hour chimes.

You have lit the fire in my soul;
Your love the ignition to my heart;
Your kiss has left its mark;
This to you; I must impart.

You are very special to me;
Missing you is another way;
To tell you that 'I love you';
So much more I want to say.

You are so incredibly handsome;
I love those beautiful eyes;
They sparkle; like precious gems;
You are a truly amazing guy.

I want you to know the real me;
I want to feel your lips on mine;
To taste the nectar of heaven;
When are mouths entwine.

You know love when you find it;
You smile & you brighten my day;
Ever since I first laid eyes on you;
I've never wanted to look away.

It's almost two in the morning;
My thoughts are all of you;
All I'm doing in my bed is turning;
& I wonder if you think of me too.

Have you ever thought twice?
About how much 'I love you'?
You are my every thing;
What else can I say or do?

You've had a profound impact on me;
You don't even need to speak;
All you have to do is smile;
& I just go weak.

You make me love my name;
Just because you say it;
Makes me feel wonderful again;
I have to admit.

You are that special guy in my heart;
Someone like you is hard to find;
You make me love you;
You are always on my mind.

You know when you are in love;
It's a feeling like no other;
'I love you Handsome';
I give you my all.

I love your beautiful eyes;
So captivating; so warm;
My favourite place to be;
Lost in their exquisite form.

You are like a star; bright & far;
When you smile;
The whole world stops & stares;
God's greatest creation; was you.

When I look at you handsome;
There's not a thing I'd change;
Because you are so amazing;
Just the way you are.

Love can touch us once;
& last for a lifetime;
Even though our paths may realign;
Our lives will be forever intertwined.

Loving you is the best feeling;
My skin longs to feel your touch;
My eyes want to gaze into yours;
I want to fall into your arm; so much.

I love you with all my might;
I dream of you when I sleep at night;
I think of you when I hug my pillow tight;
I'm so happy when you come into sight.

Your eyes are so beautiful; so warm;
They sparkle; they twinkle;
I get lost in them;
You could be 'Rip Van Winkle'.

You are everything a girl could want;
You are so handsome & charismatic;
I cherish every second with you;
When I'm with you; I'm ecstatic.

God made you handsome;
Then he made me;
Then he whispered;
'Meant to be'.

So many words in my heart;
That is still unspoken;
All that I have given away;
Can never be broken.

Never doubt my love for you;
You will always be in my heart;
Till the end of time;
Of this I'm sure & impart.

No matter the hour;
No matter the time;
You are always;
Always on my mind.

At night I lay awake;
Thinking thoughts of you;
I wonder if you are awake;
Thinking of me too.

I know one day; no matter what;
Of my adorations you will tire;
You'll grow weary of my feelings for you;
& no longer will I be required.

Life will separate us;
We'll end up in different places;
But I hope wherever you are;
What we had; you'll always embrace.

I love you Handsome;
I will love you forever;
As I hand you my heart;
Forsaking you never.

You intimated my attraction is lust;
A sinful, sensuous appetite;
A desire to satisfy a bodily need;
A feeling that fades with time!

If you were even half right;
I'd have given up a long time ago;
Dropping off your radar;
A now non-existent blimp!

Never judge a book by its cover;
Rarely are things what they seem;
Sometimes a really simple cover;
Can hide a beautiful story.

I may not be a beauty Queen;
Nor am I a best seller;
Remove my ordinary cover however;
You'll be surprised what's underneath.

My heart is made of solid gold;
I'd give you the shirt off my back;
Jeans may be my favourite apparel; and
Barefoot my footwear of choice.

But if you ever want someone to love you;
I'll always be there for you;
Be it today, tomorrow or whenever;
My love for you will never die.

You are like the sun;
You bring shine to my life everyday;
I want you to look into my eyes;
& never look away.

Look into my eyes handsome;
& tell me what you see;
You are my passion for life;
& the fire burning inside me.

When you smile handsome;
Even the sun gets jealous;
Hence how can I be blamed?
For being overzealous.

I know I can't ever lose;
What I can't ever own;
But my love for you;
I have to make known.

Love is just a word;
You give it definition;
My feelings for you;
I've made my admissions.

You are the compass of my life;
Without you, I'm lost;
Upon my heart; your name;
I have forever embossed.

It's you;
You mean everything to me;
So much more than my words;
I'm in love with you, can't you see?

You seem to find it hard to believe;
That I could love you as I do;
I wish I could prove to you;
My love for you is real & true.

You have an Angelic face;
With a smile brighter than sun light;
I love your twinkling eyes;
More beautiful than the stars at night.

Every time I look into your eyes;
They speak a thousand things;
Exotic & exquisitively beautiful;
They virtually sing.

There will always be a place;
Deep down in my heart;
A special place where only you;
Will occupy that part.

You are a wonderful person;
& that is true;
There's no one else in the world;
That I desire more than you!

Two paths crossed one fateful day;
One was yours; the other mine;
Two souls seeking affection;
Hence God decreed our paths align.

You are a truly special guy;
You're too amazing for me;
You've made me the girl;
I never thought I'd be.

I recall the way your body felt;
As I held you close to me;
In my heart & soul;
Is where you will always be.

The flickering of the candle;
Danced upon your skin;
My fingers memorised your body;
& I fell in love all over again.

You instantly brighten a room;
You are a precious gift to me;
Oh, I love you so very much;
Alas, this dream can never be.

My ring less finger says I'm single;
But that's not actually true;
My heart does belong to someone;
& that someone is YOU!

You are the most gorgeous creature;
God has ever put on this Earth;
No one & nothing comes close to you;
You have no idea of your worth.

You are the sunshine;
That makes the whole world shine;
You shine; inside & out;
So much love & beauty, entwined.

I love the way that the light;
Glistens in your beautiful eyes;
Like the moon shining out at night;
& as bright as the morning sky.

When you held me tight; so close;
I could feel your heart beat;
I melted down like a candle;
When our souls finally met.

I love everything about you;
From your personality to your eyes;
Even though I can't ever have you;
I will never question why.

When my mobile rings;
I light up like a burning candle;
I hope & pray it will be you;
Something I must learn to handle.

You may not know this;
I'm writing this just to say;
I love you with all my heart & soul;
& I will till my last day.

You are so beautiful;
Your touch; your lips; your smell;
Your beauty; your mind; your softness;
Something's you just can't sell.

Like the stars need light;
You are a ray of sunshine;
Sunshine lighting up the world;
What you are . . . divine.

Every time I look into your eyes;
I'm drawn into their intensity;
I would love to stay there forever;
Some might call this a propensity.

Love is a feeling; a connection;
A bond; when distance puts us apart;
Love is when; you just know;
The ache I get in my heart.

You bring a happiness to me;
When you're by my side;
The kind, gentle person you are;
When you open your arms out wide.

Yesterday was history;
Today is a gift;
Tomorrow is a mystery;
I fear one day you'll set me adrift.

I have been touched by an Angel;
My life will never be the same;
My life was like a thunderstorm;
Until into it you came.

When you touch me & we kiss;
You take me to paradise;
There's not another feeling;
Which can compare or suffice.

I love the way my tiny hands;
Fit so snugly inside yours;
Always so warm; so gentle;
They were made for mine; I'm sure.

In my lifetime, I have looked;
Into the eyes of many a man;
None have touched my heart & soul;
The way your eyes can.

Like the clouds love a mountaintop;
& the desert loves the rain;
I love you with all my heart & soul;
& forever within; you will remain.

They say 'seeing is believing';
That first day I saw you;
I stopped doubting;
I did & that's true.

Seven Wonders of the World there were;
Then the world saw your smile & laugh;
The seven wonders turned to eight;
No one can compete; on your path.

Your beautiful smile teases me;
Your laugh tempts me to start;
Your captivating eyes hypnotise me;
Your voice warms my heart.

Like the moon lights up the night;
You have a wonderful smile;
A smile that makes others beam;
& makes my life worthwhile.

Like a beautiful shooting star; or
An oyster adorned with a white pearl;
Don't let the world change your smile;
Let your smile change the world.

I can't stop showing this love;
That comes from within;
So strong & so passionate;
I pray it never wears thin.

I've never known anyone like you;
So soft & gentle; big in stature;
You are an incredible lover;
Sending me into raptures.

Like a soft, gentle breeze;
On a beautiful summer's day;
Secure & warm; like your arms;
It reminds me of you; I can say.

Like a loud clap of thunder;
Unexpected & often unseen too;
My heart races; my breath held;
Just as they do, when I'm with you.

I could never hate you handsome;
& please never feel bad;
My love for you is unconditional;
No matter what; I won't get made.

I so wish you would miss me though;
Alas, I know you don't have time;
I will never stop loving you;
In my eyes; you will always shine.

I love you my Angel;
You are so beautiful in every way;
God combined all your qualities;
You have your own unique way.

All I say & all that I do;
Revolves around my loving you;
Nobody is special to me except you;
I love you so much, it's really true.

I love your precious smile;
I love the way you make me feel;
I love the way you kiss me;
My delight; I just can't conceal.

When you place my hand in yours;
I feel instantly at peace;
I never want to let you go;
Our grasp, I don't want to release.

Your beauty is so fine;
So fine I just can't define;
You are so deep & sweet & kind;
My Angel; you literally shine.

Deep inside my heart;
I know that you are there;
I'll never let go; not even for a day;
My love; no need to further declare.

Destiny decides who touches our life;
Your heart decides who touches your soul;
Keeping your feelings from someone; is
A great mistake; but one you can control.

I love you more than life itself;
Since the first time I spoke your name;
Instant feelings of emotions came;
I believe destiny is the one to blame.

God put you here for a reason; that's me
No one can ever love you the way I do;
Just sit back, watch, wait & see;
I promise to always be true.

Your radiant smiles irreplaceable;
I'd travel around the world a million times;
Just to look into your beautiful eyes;
How I try to tell you through my rhymes.

You are truly one-of-a-kind;
You are the beat to my heart;
You are the air I breathe;
When we're apart; the beat doesn't start.

So I just want you to know;
Since you first entered my view;
Life is so much sweeter because . . . .
I've been in love with you.

It's a crime to denounce the beauty;
Of a creature such as thee;
To simply castaway the precision;
God placed in forging you . . . see.

For you define beauty;
In both body & mind;
Your soft & gentle face;
More beauty I'll never find.

You're my handsome poetic God;
Enveloped in a veil of excellence;
You are so beautiful, amazing & special;
Coupled with your intelligence.

You are a bright star;
That brightens my dull night;
You are the sun;
That makes my dawn more bright.

My love for you is indescribable;
You were truly sent from God above;
You are my Angel;
Sent to teach my how to love.

How I want you to look at me;
The same way I look at you;
The day I met you;
Was a dream come true.

There is nothing more beautiful in nature;
Than God's creation of you;
There is nothing more vivid;
Than my nightly dreams of you; it's true.

There is nothing more spectacular;
Than looking into your beautiful eyes;
There is no greater sensation;
Than that your touch applies.

There is nothing more delicious;
Than the taste of your kiss;
Nothing better than holding your hand;
Now that is something I really miss.

There is nothing I long for more;
Than the sound of your voice;
There is nothing that delights greater;
Than a call/text from you; made by choice.

There is no greater pleasure;
Than seeing you smile;
There is nothing more perfect;
Than lying next to you; if only for a while.

There are no words that can express;
The way I feel when I am with you;
There is no feelings that can describe;
Just what it is that you do . . . (to me).

How I long for your love & attention;
Knowing that it can never be;
There is no greater love that you will see;
Than the love that I have for you within me.

The love of my life;
Just dumped me via text;
What a cowardly act;
He just wanted sex.

I gave him my heart;
Right from the start;
Looking back now;
That wasn't that smart.

Others were easy to let go;
Eros . . . . He was not;
He is everywhere I look;
. . . . call it besot.

A book of love letters written;
A folder of poems;
All a waste of time;
Like useless sandy loom.

Showered with gifts of love;
A multitude of cards;
I didn't realise then;
Loving him would be so hard.

Yes I feel cheated;
Yes I feel used;
Left all alone now;
Emotionally abused.

I pray he finds happiness;
I pray he finds peace;
For me however . . . .
Never a release.

My life changed forever;
27 . . . . 10 . . . . 2011;
When, dumped via a text;
Hey!, this isn't heaven.

What can be said about this man?
That ends a love in this way;
Lots of words come to mind;
None on this site I can say.

Face to face would take courage;
Over the phone . . . . respect;
Neither were forthcoming;
What did I expect?

Bedazzled by his handsomeness;
Captivated by his charm;
Engrossed within his eyes,
Missed the sign—'Incoming Harm'.

Left to cry alone;
Mobile phone disconnected;
Hell! What was I thinking?
Again . . . . expected.

I thought he was special;
My soul mate; the one;
All he was looking for:
A little fun.

Now I'm left to ponder;
If things differently I'd one;
He is the loser here;
Gone!—his chosen one.

Days fade into days;
Nights; longer & longer;
I can only pray now;
This leaves me the stronger.

Dams of water I've cried;
My heart is still bleeding;
God I wish he . . . .
This poem he was reading.

What do I feel for him now?
Sympathy;
Lots of love; and
Empathy.

I believe now;
Never again will I see;
The love of my life;
Hell! It was what was to be.

If I had known then;
What I know now;
Would I have done anything differently?
How ???

Trapped now in anger;
Left to cry in pain;
I am left wondering;
What did he have to gain?

I wonder if he knows;
My life will never be the same;
Or if he even cares;
Or was it all just a game.

Poetry is . . . .
My way of grieving;
A way to express;
Hell! I am seething.

You always hurt;
The one you love;
Or so they say;
Why me? . . . . Heaven above.

My love is repressed by anger;
My heart battered & bleeding;
What can fix this?
No amount of reading.

He wasn't the man;
I thought him to be;
I guess only time; and
We will see.

I will always love him;
A promise I will keep;
It is somewhat difficult;
When all you do is weep.

I've never fell for anyone;
The way I feel for this man;
He touched me in many ways;
I pray one day I can.

I still love him;
More & more each day;
I must be stupid;
That's all I can say.

My Guardian Angel;
Please watch over me;
It is a difficult time;
For me now; you see.

It's like I'm all alone;
I have no one to turn to;
What do I do?
If I cant have you.

He was my best friend;
He was my soul mate;
He was my love;
Now it's too late.

He wasn't the man;
I thought him to be;
Dumped by SMS;
Why didn't I see?

You gave my heart;
A second chance;
You gave my soul;
A reason to dance.

Because of you;
I found a backbone;
Then you went & left me;
Sadly, all alone.

Thanks to you;
I found self pride;
But you made it;
One hell of a ride.

You left me alone;
Took the easy way out;
Went to another;
I just want to shout.

You left me feeling;
Abandoned & alone;
No longer needing;
To sit by the phone.

I pray that one day;
You'll return to my door;
But you'll have to;
Pick me up off the floor.

I still hear his words;
Inside my head;
Boy I was clearly;
Clearly, misled.

As the summer leaves fall;
And grace the grass below;
As the birds above;
Put on a lovemaking show.

As a myriad of flowers bloom;
Into an abundance of life;
Beauty it seems;
Is abundantly rife.

Life should be great;
And full of happiness too;
But losing you;
Crying is all I can do.

I gave you my every thing;
I held nothing back;
But courage you obviously;
Obviously lack.

I deserved better;
After all that we shared;
Face to face;
Would have been only fair.

But you chose a text;
A gutless way to go;
Obviously no ramifications;
An all time low.

Always in his thoughts;
He said I always was;
How he missed me too;
All these words because . . . ?

He told me he cared;
Other terms of endearment said;
All he wanted . . . ;
He and me in bed.

In order to protect him;
Our secret I kept;
If others only knew;
With me he'd slept.

I gave him more of me;
Then I have to any other;
I'm not sure I can ever;
Give this love to another.

He has a million dollar smile;
That made me melt away;
I love him more than anything;
What more need I say?

I know I should hate him;
But that's just not me;
He's no idea what he's lost;
With me what he could be.

Forgiving is easy;
Forgetting . . . . the hard part;
Forever he will be;
Inside my heart.

He will always be;
The most important person to me;
I will always wonder;
Why he could not see.

Love is a gift from God;
Love just doesn't run away;
I will always wonder why;
With me he could not stay.

I told him of my feelings;
But he started the affection;
Abandoning me however . . . .
Not the way or correction.

I know for the time being;
I have to let him go;
I pray that one day;
Back in my life he'll show.

I just wanted to love him;
He was afraid to love me too;
There's so much of me to love;
But he'll never know . . . . so.

I pray he is happy now;
And finds his dream;
Anything he needs;
To make him continue to beam.

I wanted to write a poem for you;
But I know it won't change anything;
You moved on & went to your wife;
Leaving me here with nothing.

You left me here with nothing more;
Than a broken heart;
And some memories I want to;
Tear apart.

You did text me . . . . Love you xxx
And that you actually cared;
You said you would never hurt me;
But trust me; I was prepared.

All my life I braced myself;
For the goodbye;
I knew it would come sooner or later;
And I knew I would cry.

Now the day has come where you crushed;
My hopes & dreams;
I hope you're happy now;
Knowing I'm crying myself to sleep.

This poem to you is nothing more than;
Goodbye;
A goodbye to the future—me and you;
Could have had.

So goodbye my Prince Charming;
Goodbye my best friend;
That's all I have to say;
Here comes the end.

Some days are okay;
Some days I'm really sad;
Some days I cope;
Some days are really bad.

Does he know I'm struggling?
Does he even care?
I wonder if he thinks of me;
And those times we shared.

I've tried every thing I can;
To forget about him too;
The way he no longer wants me;
What else can I do?

He left an incredible mark;
On my heart & soul;
Without him in my life;
I'm left with a gapping hole.

He was a rival competitor;
He initiated the first kiss;
I wasn't totally innocent;
Boy! It's him that I miss.

I was probably just another;
Notch on his gun;
All he wanted . . . ;
Just a little fun.

I pray one day he realises;
That I meant something to him;
He seeks me out to rekindle;
A love with him to begin.

Now I know how it feels;
To be alone & astray;
Forced away by the one I love;
Made to go away.

He once said that he couldn't;
Do the physical without the emotional;
Now I have come to realise;
For him; it was purely recreational.

I once asked him;
Why he didn't push me away;
He said that I was special;
And that he wanted me to stay.

He used to call me 'Gorgeous';
He told me I was 'a gift';
So why then?
Did he set me adrift?

I pray each & everyday that;
I'm having a nightmare;
And that I will awaken soon; and
Our lives together we will share.

I only ever asked one thing of him;
To never lose me from his life;
He said I'd never lose him;
You could have cut me with a knife.

Today is two weeks since he;
Told me he couldn't stay in touch;
Despite saying I wouldn't lose him;
Did I ask too much?

He will never again know;
A love so deep;
A passion so great; and
That I'd do anything; it to keep.

You'll run out of words to say;
He used to joke with me;
How wrong he was; I hope;
One day these poems he does read.

Be patient I'm told;
One day this man;
He will return to you; and
Take you by the hand.

I never once said no to him;
Nor would that I ever do;
It's a pity the same can't be said;
Of him to and for me too.

Despite everything; my love;
Will never fade with time;
That's why it's so easy;
My poems to him; do rhyme.

I wonder if he thinks of me.
The way I think of him;
He's constantly on my mind;
I'd rather have lost a limb.

I hope the gifts I gave him;
Reminds him of me;
Each and every time he;
Walks past them and sees.

I close my eyes and remember;
Its 09-06-2011;
The Hotel room;
He came and took me to heaven.

He performed like a God;
He knew exactly what to do;
To make me feel loved and wanted;
As I tried to do for him too.

Whenever he could see me;
I let 'nothing' stand in our way;
Cancelled appointments and commitments;
Without knowing this; he pushed me away.

I never ever misled him;
I never told him a lie;
The same can't be said of him;
Why the disparity? Why?

You told me you're letting me go;
The tears I shed for you;
Wasn't something I wanted to happen?
And it still is not.

I never deserted or left your side;
You pushed me away;
I never lied to you;
Why didn't you stay?

I never made you cry;
You sure made me cry though;
I can't believe you cut me;
You've made me feel so low.

I love you so much;
Like the sun loves noon;
I love you so much;
Like the night loves the moon.

I miss you so much;
But you don't want me;
You broke my heart;
Why can't you see?

I love you so much;
God I miss your touch;
I miss your voice; your calls;
God, this isn't just.

I am so sad;
I am so mad;
Was I just a fad?
Was I all that bad?

I will never regret what we had;
I'd do it all over again;
It was so incredibly special;
I'd do anything to regain the same.

Did I give my love too easy?
Did I give my heart too soon?
Did I give my soul without question?
I believed we were in tune.

Did he love me at all?
Did he even care?
Did I mean anything to him?
What about what we shared?

As the stars shone in his eyes;
As the warmth came from his touch;
As his smile lit up the night;
I thought we had so much.

Was I a fool?
Was idiot on my forehead?
Am I just stupid?
Why didn't I see where this lead?

Were his touches misleading?
Were his words all lies?
When I was with him;
I felt like I could fly.

I will always remember him;
I will always have those memories;
Of those times that we shared;
Written in poems in my diaries.

I love you my special man;
But I have to let you go;
You don't want me anymore;
It's going to be tough though.

If only you'd have known;
'Love' is my middle name;
Hell! What could have been?
It's such a dam shame.

There will never be another you;
God couldn't make two like you;
Lots will try and fail;
To you; I'll always be true.

If things had been different;
It would have been something special;
How I just loved it;
When we would nestle.

You will always be with me;
I'll never meet another like you;
If only you'd felt;
The same about me too.

I hope one day you read these;
And I pray that you do;
And from my words you see;
My love for you is true.

If only you'd have really known;
The love inside me for you;
If only you could have shown me;
A little love from you too.

I've never before written like this;
I'd struggle with just a card;
For you the words flow freely;
It definitely isn't hard.

When I lost you handsome;
My whole world fell apart;
I'd only have to think of you;
For the tears to start.

A deluge of tears I've cried;
Since you told me goodbye;
You said I'd never lose you;
This was just another lie.

Although it's been weeks now;
You are always on my mind;
Just look in my heart;
Love for you you'll always find.

My heart you did break;
Me; you did devastate;
I still don't believe it;
I thought you were my mate.

I pray one day my phone will ring;
Or you suddenly appear at my door;
No questions will be asked;
I could not ask for more.

The cards say you'll come;
Some hurdles you have to beat;
The next 30 years together;
Getting you here; the feat.

You are my perfect man;
Of that I have no doubt;
If I had you handsome;
I would have to shout.

Such an array of words;
Over a protracted period of time;
Must convince you of my love;
And that for you it shines.

Any other woman;
Would have given up by now;
But I live in hope;
One day you'll find how.

I promise you'll never regret it;
You will want for nothing;
Your every wish fulfilled;
All the while; I'll be gushing.

I can't believe you walked away;
After all that we shared;
I would be totally devastated;
If I though you never cared.

Your words indicated you cared;
Your actions showed emotion;
Was I just foolish to think?
That you might care; a notion.

I can't believe you faked it;
Your hand quivering a sign;
That during our times together;
You wanted to be mine.

You were always sweet & tender;
Ever the gentleman; caring;
Always ensuring;
Our love making was sharing.

I loved the way always after;
Within your arms you'd hold me;
Your embrace all-encompassing;
Nowhere else did I want to be?

You gave me so much of you;
Then you took it all away;
I would have paid any price;
If you would have stayed.

But every time you walked away;
All alone I was left to be;
Being the 'other woman';
Is not an easy place to be?

You couldn't give me what I wanted;
You said you'd never hurt me;
But you took everything on offer;
Then via a text; set me free.

You took the easy way out;
You didn't have to face me;
To tell me it was fun while it lasted;
But my tears you didn't want to see.

I gave you far more credit;
Than this cowardly gesture deserves;
I pray some day you get the courage;
To tell me face to face; despite the nerves.

Despite everything that's happened;
I love you more and more;
I'd take you back tomorrow;
And not want to even the score.

I knew from the very start;
No matter what; I'd come in second;
You didn't have any other choice;
That's what I reckon.

I'd do it all over again;
Knowing the outcome would be the same;
You were worth all the hurt and pain;
We both must share the blame.

I wonder do you ever ponder.
Why I didn't attempt to stay in touch?
After all my words and deeds;
That said I love you so very much.

I can assure you it isn't easy;
Nor each day the desire gets less;
It takes every ounce of courage;
My life without you; it's a mess.

Nothing takes the pain away;
Not even a little;
I've tried everything I can;
Even tried playing the fiddle.

I pray you know I'm hurting;
I hope one day you right the wrong;
I guess only time will tell;
Perhaps when you listen to my song.

I gave you numerous gifts of love;
That, if kept, you would sometimes see;
I hope and pray to God each day;
That one day they remind you of me.

There must have been something;
That kept you coming back;
But then again you did;
Essentially, give me the sack.

Poetry is my way to express;
All the hurt that I feel;
Because you handsome;
My heart you did steal.

You told me you missed me;
And I was always in your thoughts;
My love was given freely;
It didn't have to be bought.

I can forgive you but;
I'd like one day to know the reason;
Why you broke your promise;
Leaving me with a permanent lesion.

Friday was thirteen weeks;
Since 'that text' . . . a few;
Lesser women would have,
Dropped you in a queue.

But in you I see someone special;
Someone who's worth the wait;
Someone who is incredible;
Someone bought together by fate.

One day you will thank me;
One day you will know;
This love that is inside me;
Yearning to get out.

Only then you will realise;
Just what you have in me;
You'll wonder why you waited;
With me . . . . to be.

I love you Beautiful;
I will never love like this again;
No man will or ever can;
Make me feel the same.

You said you'd never hurt me;
But you did . . . ;
You said I'd never lose you;
Again, . . . but I did.

I love you Beautiful;
I wish every time I say it;
It echoed in your head;
And you regret you quit.

Looking at you; is looking;
At one of the most beautiful;
Sites there are in the world;
And that's no bull.

I am not angry;
I am not bitter;
I don't want revenge; but
I wish I didn't feel like litter.

You lifted me up;
From the deepest place;
Then you pulled the rug out; and
Allowed me to fall on my face.

Do you know what's sad?
I'm still in love with you;
Do you know what's sadder!
You don't care too.

You will always be special to me;
I love you so very much;
Despite the fact that you;
No longer want to remain in touch.

You were there when I needed you;
And there was a reason we were to bond;
God brought us together for a reason;
For the two of us to grow fond.

I love you my special guy;
You'll never know just how much;
You played me for a fool;
And I as an easy touch.

You got everything you wanted;
You never had to ask twice;
All I wanted was to please you;
And the experience to be nice.

All the hours of the night;
Words of adoration come to mind;
Thinking of you makes it easy;
And words of love easy to find.

Out of sight; out of mind;
I doubt you even think of me;
How different it is for me though;
I'm always thinking of thee.

You have no idea of what you had;
I'd have given you anything;
Anything at all for the asking;
Absolutely everything . . . .

I gave you my heart;
I surrendered you my soul;
It turned out however;
I was just your mole.

I hope you can live with yourself;
And that you hurt me so bad;
Ever since you cut me out;
I have been constantly sad.

But you don't have a worry;
You can forget I exist;
And everything we had and shared;
Now just a distant mist.

You were on a win—win;
I was on a lose—lose;
The only good thing however;
Only you got to choose.

I was a dam fool;
But I'd do it all again;
Only this time;
Your affection I'd try to retain.

It was always when you wanted it;
You held all the aces;
I was left;
Chasing behind six paces.

You promised many coffees;
You promised many dinners;
Only a few came to fruition;
You; always the winner.

I don't know how many times;
Your broken promises left me hanging;
An often-feeble excuse given;
Leaving me for you; panging.

You did it to me all too often;
It was probably just a game;
No matter the reason;
You will never again treat me the same.

I stare out the window and wonder;
What are you doing today?
And if our paths ever recrossed;
What? If anything, you'd say.

I'd hope that you'd apologise;
For how you mistreated me;
I guess only time will tell;
I'll have to wait and see.

It would be great if you'd concede;
What you did was wrong;
And I'd probably let you off;
If you did it in a song.

In time; your photograph will fade;
But the memories will live on;
Deep inside my heart;
Where they will always belong.

You said you didn't doubt my feelings;
Not even for a second;
Probably more of your bullshit;
That's what I reckon.

Every time I hear a Kookaburra laugh;
I think it is laughing at me;
And the total fool I was;
To fall in love with you; you see.

I pray that you never feel;
This used and alone;
After all that we shared;
To be devastated via phone.

Looking back in hindsight;
All your words were just crap;
So around your little finger;
Me you could wrap.

Please God give me the strength;
To get through this difficult time;
Since I lost you handsome;
I've forgotten how to shine.

Sometimes letting go;
Is the hardest thing to do?
I've found out how true this is;
Since I've lost you.

Sometimes you don't realise;
The precious things we had;
Until we have lost them;
And appreciate it wasn't a fad.

Please God help me;
I don't know what to do;
I want to keep reaching out;
For you; to you.

We did find happiness handsome;
In each others arms;
I gave you everything I had to offer;
Not realising it'd end in my harm.

My life's now a roller coaster;
A ride of ups and downs;
Since I've lost you;
Stability just can't be found.

I sit here and think about you;
All I can do is cry;
Coping would be easier;
If only I knew why.

The tears they just stream;
Stream down my face;
I just can't stop them;
Crying; not a Case with grace.

I feel like I've lost everything;
You were everything to me;
I love you Handsome;
If only you could see.

It's because I love you;
All I can think about is you;
Do you ever?
Think about me too.

I know that God;
Holds you in his hand;
I know he will cushion you;
No matter where you land.

My darkness has deepened;
Since I've lost you;
You had your cake & the icing;
All about you; all you.

I've never felt so weak;
I can't bear another day;
Without you in my life;
So much still left to say.

Why should I spend another moment?
Watching you drift further away;
I would have paid any price;
If with me; you would have stayed.

I hope the list of my weaknesses;
Will help you become strong;
Loving you Handsome;
Was anything but wrong.

Even if you lose the one you love;
You must never turn away;
We must keep them in our hearts;
And the memories there will stay.

I will never forget you;
For as long as I live;
All I ever wanted from you;
Just a little . . . give.

Without you I'm lost;
The hole it's left in my heart;
Can never be repaired;
To the way it was at the start.

Just the thought of you;
Still brings me to tears;
All the time we shared together;
Losing you, my greatest fear.

When you lose the one you love;
You never really get over it;
You just carry on; and
You learn to live with the 'hit'.

I love you Gorgeous;
I love you so much;
I wanted to give you everything;
Whilst keeping my love for you . . . hush, hush.

As I look out at the sky so blue;
My thoughts drift back to you;
All the memories we shared;
Of all that we did do.

When I look at the grass so green;
I think of your beautiful eyes;
How I loved looking into them;
As they sparkled like the night skies.

When I close my eyes at night;
I remember your beautiful kiss;
And how it could transport me;
To a place of extreme bliss.

I recall the way your touch;
Would make my body shake;
And how I'd ask you to pinch me;
To ensure that I was awake.

All I need Handsome;
Is your hand to hold;
You can't tell me;
That you haven't been told.

Its been months now; and
I still write poems to you each day;
You must ask yourself;
What does this say?

It's been months now but;
You're always in my thoughts;
Feelings like this;
Just can't be bought.

You said you'd never hurt me;
When it was inevitable;
Like 'you're not going to lose me';
Of it . . . . you were full.

Naked in the pouring rain I stand;
To wash thoughts of you away;
Nothing I do works however;
Within my head and heart you stay.

I know it took two of us;
To make our feelings shown;
But you had all the say;
In where and when it had grown.

You could have stopped it anytime;
You always had the power;
It might have been better if;
You'd placed me alone in a tower.

When I said I'd never hurt you;
I meant each and every word;
For me to deliberately hurt you;
Would be simply absurd.

You are the moon;
The lover that I lost;
The birds sing for your return;
At absolutely any cost.

I recall the way my body;
Would fit nicely into yours;
When I think about those memories;
My feelings they do soar.

Every night I ask the Angels;
To lead you back to me;
I pray that they are listening;
I'll just have to wait and see.

You made me feel special;
You made me feel worthwhile;
You made me feel like someone;
Just look at the smile on my dial.

You'll never know how you hurt me;
You'll never know how much I cared;
You'll never know how much I prayed;
For a life together . . . . shared.

I've told you in a million words;
Shown you in a thousand ways;
Of the love that I have for you;
What more can I possibly say?

You chose to walk away;
Couldn't face me to my face;
I thought you were a better man;
One with much more grace.

You obviously had your reasons;
I pray one day those you'll disclose;
On one knee & between your teeth;
Carrying a beautiful rose.

I wish you were here right now;
Together we'd listen to the rain;
Loving you with such passion;
Some would call me insane.

I've tried to walk away;
I've tried to let you go;
There are to many coincidences;
To you I'd love to show.

Do you believe in coincidence?
Do you believe in fate?
I believe God brought us together;
He handed me to you on a plate.

A turning point in my life;
Was falling in love with you;
My life will never be the same;
I pray you feel that way too.

I guess I'll never really know;
Just what you truly felt;
If you had feelings for me;
That would cause you to melt.

The cards say we'll be together;
My heart tells me—no way!
That's why you cut me off;
With me; you could not stay.

You are so incredibly beautiful;
I couldn't stop staring at you;
I found you were more beautiful;
On the inside too.

I love you Beautiful;
But my love wasn't enough;
I know that leaving me;
For you; had to be tough.

I sit and cry a lot;
My thought filled only of you;
What more could I have done?
To make you love me too.

I know that thousands of words;
Are not enough to tell you;
My hearts feelings; my emotions;
And my passion towards you too.

If tomorrow never comes;
Will you know how much I love you?
I have tried in every way;
To tell you each and everyday.

You are a gift from God;
And 'I love you';
More than anything in the world;
My special someone; its true.

When I see your smiling face;
All my troubles melt away;
When you take me in your arms;
There's not a word you need to say.

Like the clouds were made to rain;
Like the sun was made to shine;
The stars were made to wish upon;
How I wish you could be mine.

To share your tender heart;
The warmness of your smile;
The courage of your wisdom;
For these I'd walk for miles.

Every time I see you;
I want you more and more;
Every time you say 'hi' to me;
My heart begins to soar.

Every time you touch me;
I pinch myself to see if I'm awake;
Every time you look into my eyes;
It's my heart that's yours to take.

Warmth spreads through me at your touch;
Love spreads through me from your kiss;
All I can think is 'I love you so much';
And when you're not with me, it's you I miss.

You can't deny we have a chemistry;
Each moment intensifies the need to touch;
Yours are the arms I want to hold me;
Oh, 'I love you' so much.

You create a spark in my heart;
Basking in the warmth of your smile;
Started a fire that is unquenchable;
And you're oh so witty style.

I'll never love anyone;
As much as I love you;
And if I ever lost you;
I don't know what I'd do.

Each night I pray to God;
That he watch over you;
To keep you safe and happy;
Do you do this for me to?

Each night I ask my Angels;
To convey my love to you;
Despite being discarded;
Like a worn out old shoe.

God gives us people;
People that we need;
Making us the person we are;
This you must concede.

Women's strengths amaze men;
We hold happiness, love and joy;
Even though men do their best;
Our love they do destroy.

We smile when we want to scream;
And sing when we want to cry;
All the rules of nature;
A woman will defy.

Our love is unconditional;
We fight for what we believe in;
Men have no idea of how easy;
Our love they can win.

We have but one flaw;
It's that we forget our worth;
Believing what others say;
Worthless, like an old girth.

I found someone special;
But he didn't want me;
I don't have to tell you;
You are the only one I see.

There isn't a day go by;
That I don't think about you;
That I don't cry out your name; and
Profess my love for you too.

I love you Handsome;
It just can be defined;
What's been shared?
Between your heart and mine.

I miss the sound of your voice;
How I miss your touch;
I miss being with and near you;
So, so very much.

I wish that you could look;
Deep inside my heart;
And see what I feel for you;
And have from the start.

It seems like I always fall short;
Of being worthy;
I always seem to run second;
I am anything but sturdy.

Some people make the world;
A much better place;
Just be being in it;
With you, that is the case.

As the sun comes up in the morning;
So do my hopes and dreams;
That one day you'll return to me;
And forever on; make me beam.

Deep in my heart though;
I know you just used me;
Took everything you wanted;
My love for you; gave you the key.

I doubt I ever cross your mind;
Though you are constantly on mine;
Despite you're loving and leaving;
I pray to God that you are fine.

You see; I would never do to you;
What you did to me;
Broken promises and words;
I pray that one day you see.

The pain and hurt you caused me;
It never had to be;
If only you had 'manned up';
You wouldn't have hurt me.

I guess I only saw in you;
What I wanted to see;
Looking back now;
You didn't have feelings for me.

If you can read my poems and;
Not be impressed by my work;
And realise the depth of my love;
Then you must be a jerk.

If you truly loved me;
Then show me respect;
The respect that I deserve;
My life you did affect.

My greatest fear was;
The fear of losing you;
My life will never be the same;
Without you in it too.

I don't want to be hurt;
That bad; ever again;
My feelings for anyone else;
I intend to restrain.

I opened up my heart to you;
I placed my soul at your feet;
You cant deny that our feelings;
Did produce an incredible heat.

I still can't believe;
That you would just walk away;
After everything we shared;
I feel like I'm the only one to pay.

Months since I've seen you;
Weeks since we've spoke;
Until the end of time;
You will be the only bloke.

Sometimes I sit and ponder;
Just what could have been?
If only you'd had the courage;
If only you could have seen.

You don't kiss someone by mistake;
Your arms didn't find me in error;
The beautiful moments we shared;
But you chose to run in terror.

Although my heart grieves for you;
I sincerely wish you all the best;
I pray that you are happy now;
And don't regret not coming west.

I know I could have made you happy;
You would never want for more;
I would have given you anything;
If only you'd walked thro' my door.

I guess now you'll never know;
Just what could have been?
A love more deep and true;
Its truly has to be seen.

To my heart you are my love;
To my soul you are my mate;
To my lips you are pure nectar;
To my arms you are a gate.

To my body you are enjoyment;
To my spirit you are angelic;
To my ears you are a delight;
To my memory you are a relic.

To my eyes you are spectacular;
To my touch you are soft as can be;
The beautiful connection we shared;
You were the rare key.

To me you'll always be special;
A once in a lifetime thing;
Of one thing you were right;
I wanted more than just a fling.

I want so much to be with you;
That I would grab onto any straw;
Hoping and praying everyday;
With you; I am so in awe.

I don't know why God did this to me;
I couldn't love you any more;
No matter how you calculate it;
It's more than you can score.

Those that are the hardest to love;
Need to be loved the most;
Anytime that you will let me;
I'll love you that close.

We were two lonely hearts;
That found each other;
Danced in perfect harmony;
I'll never find this with another.

I just wanted you to love me;
Not just used for your own pleasure;
I wanted you to make me see;
What I am to you; your treasure.

I wrote down in poetry;
My feelings oh so true;
Just how much I love you;
But you never cherished them too.

I still hear your voice;
As clear as it was a bell;
Since you dumped me however;
I've been through sheer hell.

I gave you absolutely everything;
And only asked you for one;
All your promises and assurances;
I might have well asked for none.

You made me cry;
You tore me apart;
You left me in tears;
You've shattered my heart.

It wasn't your fault;
I guess it was me;
For love can't be forced;
Perhaps we weren't meant to be.

It still doesn't help;
Now that I know;
Because for some reason;
My heart won't let go.

I've tried more than once;
To get over you;
But it is so very hard;
No matter what I do.

I thought love was joy;
But I've got nothing to gain;
Just sorrow and tears;
And a little more pain.

The day the pain started;
Reality came too;
It was the day I realised;
I'll never be with you.

How can I forget someone?
Who gave me so much to remember?
Even though you've let me go;
My memories glow like an ember.

Only when you hurt someone;
Do you realise they truly love you;
So if you want me in your life;
Find a way to put me there too.

In the end;
We regret the chances we don't take;
The relationships we were afraid to have;
And the decisions we waited too long to make.

When I lost you;
Both of us lost;
But you lost the most;
While I paid the biggest cost.

I just want you to be happy;
That's what you deserve;
Despite everything that's happened;
My time with you; I'll always preserve.

If my love for you was fake;
Or even let's say . . . lust;
I'd not be feeling like this today;
Surely you'd agree; you must.

I pour my heart out in words;
I can't say them to you in person;
Tears stream down my face;
My despair over you; just worsens.

My smile is a lie;
It masks and hides my pain;
And how I truly feel;
It has all been in vain.

Please look into my eyes;
And you will see the truth;
My eyes; they can only cry;
Do you need more proof?

You are the only one handsome;
The one that I love the most;
No one will ever come close;
You will be always and foremost.

Just wrap your arms around me;
And I will be all yours;
Not a question will be asked;
You can count on me for sure.

How could you just walk away?
When you knew that I loved you;
I showed you in everyway;
I thought you loved me too.

How could you just walk away?
After all the words you said;
All the times we were together;
Lying side by side in bed.

How could you just walk away?
After all that we shared;
The promises, the secrets, the words;
All of which said you cared.

How could you just walk away?
When you promised you'd stay;
In my life forever and said;
Give me time; I'll find a way.

How could you just walk away?
Without telling me to my face;
You chose the easy way out;
Wasn't that the case?

How could you just walk away?
I thought you were better than that;
I know you had your reasons;
You could have done it in a chat.

I won't do it again;
Love someone with all my heart;
So truly and unconditionally;
As I did you from the start.

I won't do it again;
So quickly declare my love;
Opening myself up for hurt;
You will always be my beloved.

I won't do it again;
Trust someone with my soul;
Giving it up without a fight;
Loving you took its toll.

I won't do it again;
Let down my guard;
Giving entry so easily;
This time it won't be a façade.

I won't do it again;
Take a chance on another;
To feel the hurt and pain again;
This time by some other.

You are the only man;
That I love and respect;
You are the only one;
With whom I did connect.

You are not like anyone;
Anyone I've ever known;
I love you Handsome;
Without you I'm so alone.

When you dumped me;
My pilot light went out;
No one else can reignite it;
Of that I have no doubt.

Since that time handsome;
My days have been dark;
My shining light gone; you
The light that left its mark.

I doubt I'll ever recover;
The pain and hurt so bad;
I can't believe the way you did it;
For that I am dam mad.

I'm not sure what the future holds;
The hurt inflicted so very deep;
The hole I need to get out of;
It's just way too steep.

I want to scream out loud;
I want to punch your chest;
I want you to know the pain;
Known by the best out west.

Why? When I get close to someone;
Do you take them away?
God, what have I done so badly?
So badly, I always have to pay.

Please believe me;
I've tried everything;
To rid you from my mind;
But nothing works; nothing.

I can't let you go; and
I won't let anyone else in;
I guess my punishment then;
Now to live with the sin.

My sin was loving you;
When you belonged to another;
I'd do it all again for you;
But not for any other.

You are truly something else;
Someone that's rare and precious;
Someone like I'll never know again;
If only you'd have been adventurous.

You never said much;
But what you did was profound;
I listened to your every word;
Lingering on your every sound.

I guess I was never good enough;
Not good enough for you;
I guess you'll never know;
Never know if its true.

I need to hear the truth;
The truth why you hurt me;
Hurt; when you promised you'd never;
I don't suppose this will ever be.

I love you Handsome;
I wish every time I said it;
That it echoed in your head;
Then you'd understand; just a bit.

If I'd never existed;
It wouldn't have made a difference;
A difference to you anyway;
In the end; you chose distance.

I will never give up hope;
That one day you'll return;
Return into my life; forever;
Only then will you truly learn.

You said 'I'm too smart for you';
You're selling yourself way short;
How can you possibly think this?
When to me; all that you've taught.

My life changed forever;
The day you came into it;
Despite everything though;
I wouldn't change a bit.

Since you set me adrift;
My life is now a sad ride;
Like a 'tinny' riding the waves;
Backwards & forward with the tide.

Thoughts of you never leave me;
My emotions ebb and flow;
I relive the memories over & over;
The tears; they come and go.

Sometimes I stop and wonder;
Why God did this to me;
It's supposed to make me stronger;
I guess I'll wait and see.

Until then handsome;
I'll take it as it comes;
The path will not be easy;
Meanwhile, I'll just remain numb.

The noblest way to be a fool;
In this lifetime;
Is to tell someone you love them;
And I've told you in words and rhyme.

I saw something on the top shelf;
When I reached up to grab it;
I realised I wasn't tall enough;
And not because I wasn't fit.

You are the man Handsome;
Whom I loved and trusted the most;
But you chose to set me adrift;
I thought that we were close.

The song lyrics say;
Our love is a child;
Fathered by a cruel man;
Yet it drives us wild.

Watch what you wish for;
Or so they say;
You could just get it;
You just may.

You break promises made;
You drink, you smoke and you lie;
And you are also good at;
By SMS saying goodbye.

I see something inside you;
Something that's great;
You can always have me;
For you, it's never too late.

Call me a fool;
Call me anything you like;
But for you Handsome;
Many miles I would hike.

You have no idea Handsome;
Just what I'd do for you;
But the question is;
Would you for me too?

Some how I don't think so;
I don't think you even care;
One day into your eyes though;
I pray I get to deeply stare.

I am being tortured;
Each and everyday;
Thoughts of you that within;
My thoughts and dreams stay.

You won't live with me handsome;
And I can't live without you;
Its 18 weeks today since we've spoke;
And I am so alone and so blue.

There is a beauty all around me;
But no matter where I look;
Its always you I see;
Your words all just gobbled gook.

My love for you Handsome;
Is poisoning me slowly;
But in my eyes;
You will always be holy.

Trust your heart;
Know the consequences;
Let down your defences;
And follow your senses.

You put a pen to my heart;
And wrote down your name;
Ever since then;
My life hasn't been the same.

You left your mark;
With every word you wrote;
All the physical attention;
And every word you spoke.

When you set me adrift;
You blew my mind;
And broke my heart in pieces;
Why was I so blind?

I didn't know I was just a character;
Another victim of your words;
Another chapter in your work;
Words & work that will never be heard.

You were the winter;
You were my shining star;
You were the writer;
That wrote off my heart.

My soul is hungry;
My heart is broken;
My love lost;
All without a word spoken.

My mind struggles to forget;
My heart won't surrender;
Not a thing I can do;
When you're the offender.

I still have trouble;
Accepting you let me go;
What we had was so special;
It was one hell of a blow.

I don't know where I stand with you;
And I don't know what I mean to you;
All I know is every time I think of you;
All I want to do is be with you.

The roses I gave you;
Was my heart in disguise?
Plant it; water it; grow it;
So it never dies.

I'm tired of portraying I'm happy;
When all I want to do is cry;
I'm tired of constantly asking;
Why? Oh my God, Why?

I can't stop wondering;
Why you hurt me;
You had to know you would;
Or could you just not see?

I thought you were different;
But you turned out not to be;
You broke my heart;
But you just can't see.

Yet you can sleep calmly;
While I'm here shedding tears;
Someone as heartless as you;
The greatest fear.

You taught me to be careful;
With who I fall for; that's
You taught me to be careful;
With whom I trust my heart.

Please God send me an Angel;
An Angel to take away the pain;
To take away the pain;
The pain that's slowly killing me;
Killing me inside.

Please God send me an Angel;
An Angel to guide me;
Guide me out of this hell;
This hell that's tearing me apart.
A hell that won't let go.

Please God send me an Angel;
An Angel to show me the way;
The way to deal with my loss;
The loss of my soul mate;
And the man that I love so much.

Please God send me an Angel;
An Angel to watch over him;
To watch over & take care of him;
From now until eternity;
Something he wouldn't let me do.

Please God send me an Angel;
An Angel to light his way;
His way to love and happiness;
For the rest of his life.
It's all I want for him.

When you left me;
A light went out in my heart;
You'll never know what you mean to me;
If only I could show you in a pie chart.

Since you left me;
My eyes can't stop crying;
My heart has shattered into pieces; and
My soul has begun slowly dying.

When you left me;
My life lost its meaning;
Nothing matters to me anymore;
My life it's now careening.

When you love someone;
It makes you weak;
Since I lost you Handsome;
My poetry, my only way to speak.

You never let me say goodbye;
I guess you had a reason;
But after all that we shared;
It felt more like treason.

Luck has never been my friend;
I am so very much alone;
I miss you so very much;
But me, you've obviously out-grown.

One simple decision;
Can change a life forever;
A decision changed my life;
The day you said our love could never.

Do you have any idea?
Just how much I love you;
I'm telling you the truth;
My heart belongs with you.

My silence is just another word;
Another word for my pain;
A love like I have for you;
I'll never, ever know again.

I sit here all alone;
Tears streaming down my face;
Perhaps Boofhead was right;
To you I'm just a disgrace.

I've been hurt before;
But nothing like I feel right now;
You let me into your heart;
But my love, you would not allow.

Love will find a way;
Even to paths where wolves fear to prey;
Wrap your arms around me & I'm whole;
But this, will you obey?

Oh my Lord God please;
Give me the strength;
To do what I need to do;
To do it at any length.

Give me the courage;
The courage to carry on;
Without the man I love and adore;
For my life; now gone.

Give me the patience;
That what I want the most;
Will come to me in God's good time;
More important and foremost.

Give me the ability;
To understand his choice;
The choice to severe me; and
Never again to hear his voice.

Give me the hope;
That one day he'll return;
Hope lives on in me forever;
To you, I appear to be no concern.

I tried following my heart;
It got me kicked in the guts;
I was left;
Feeling like a smut.

I tried being true to myself;
Opened my heart & soul to you;
But despite all that;
I've been left alone and blue.

I've tried living without regrets;
I told you how I felt;
That every time you were near me;
My heart would just melt.

I tried trusting a man again;
I beared my heart & soul to you;
I kept no secrets; not a one;
Can you say that too?

I tried loving a man again;
I held nothing back;
I gave you my all My Love;
What I got; a giant wack.

Despite all this you've given me plenty;
There'll always be a place here for you;
No matter what has happened;
My love for you will always remain true.

The last words I utter;
Before I go to sleep at night;
'I love you Handsome';
I love you with all my might.

I can only hold onto hope;
For only so long;
Why do I bother though?
When to another you belong.

I beat you never think of me;
I never cross your mind;
And should I get to ask you;
This is what I'll find.

I still can't believe you did this;
Let me go that way;
Not afford me a call or visit;
To tell me you could not stay.

I ask myself why you promised;
The things you promised me;
When you knew all along;
You'd never keep them you see.

My love for you has never waned;
Never diminished in the least;
Even though I'm left to feel;
I have been well and truly fleeced.

I love you Handsome;
I love you with all my heart;
I want you to have all you want;
I pray for you; this is a new start.

A part of me died;
The day you said goodbye;
Not a day goes by since then;
That I don't cry and cry.

Am I ever going to see your face again?
Look into those incredible eyes;
Eyes that cause my heart to melt;
Each & every time you say goodbye.

The physic read my cards;
The first seven of eight;
All love cards fell;
It is truly fate.

The next to follow;
The sunshine card;
The card of happiness;
With you; that is not hard.

She said you'd return to me;
But she couldn't say when;
I guess I'll just live in hope;
And my words I'll continue to pen.

Living life without you;
Is like living in a thick fog;
Whilst walking waist deep;
In an endless bog.

My life without you;
Has lost its meaning;
Losing your soul mate;
You just cease beaming.

Each day I drift further;
Further into an empty space;
A zone of nothingness;
I can't survive this race.

I exist;
But I don't really;
An empty shell that once was;
God I love you deeply.

You may not think so;
But you made my life complete;
However with the other;
I simply can't compete.

Each day I wonder;
How can I go on without you?
Each day is more difficult;
Believe me; it's true.

My heart is slowly dying;
My soul has lost its lustre;
It only some courage;
You could find to muster.

To face me now;
Like you should have done then;
And tell me to my face;
But will this happen? When?

Losing you;
My heart feels the pain;
I'm beginning to falter;
Under the strain.

You'll never know;
How close I came;
To just giving up;
Its such a dam shame.

Each night I pray to God;
While I lay here weeping;
That I don't see tomorrow;
That he take me while sleeping.

My soul mate;
Has been taken from me;
And for the life of me;
The reason I cannot see.

I still grieve for you Handsome;
Although months have gone by;
I grieve my loss and cry;
Still asking why God, why?

The time we spent together;
So incredible yet short;
We found in each other a soul mate;
Yet you chose to abort.

Life is just so unfair and harsh;
It took me 50+ years to find you;
You shared my life for another four;
Now I'm so miserable and blue.

You were the only good thing;
To ever come into my life;
Yet for me;
All I was to you—constant strife.

You found a good in me;
Something others chose to ignore;
Although months have passed;
I find myself wanting you more.

My only solace;
After all this time;
Are expressed in my words;
Words that flow from mine.

I go to sleep at night;
Your photograph upon my chest;
I want to tattoo your name;
Across my left breast.

Each time I cup a rosebud;
It's your face I see within;
Because inside your cards;
A dried rosebud I'd place therein.

I watch the rain outside;
Running down the window pane;
I'm reminded of my tears;
Tears I've cried for you in vain.

As I see the clouds adrift;
I see only my lost soul;
Drifting about aimlessly;
Lost within a deep hole.

I stand in the pouring rain;
To cleanse myself of you;
To rid myself of the hurt & pain;
And the ever feeling of blue.

My love for you My Love;
It knows no bounds;
If only you'd allow me;
My love for you would astound.

When I look at you handsome;
I'm looking at God's creation;
I look at you in awe;
You are such a temptation.

There isn't a tree;
So beautiful and green;
That compares to your eyes;
The most beautiful I've ever seen.

As I look at the full moon;
I'm reminded again of you;
So beautiful and so full;
All alone; amongst the blue.

My Lord thou God;
Why do I suffer so?
Day after day; night after night;
When you know I am so low.

I do love you my love;
I never really understood;
Understood until now;
If only you too would.

I can't imagine my life now;
Without you there in it;
My life is so empty;
And no longer is it brightly lit.

Standing on the platform;
The locomotive in view;
It is only a few steps;
Just a few.

My hands are shaking;
My heart beats fast;
Only a few seconds;
And it could be past.

It's only know I understand;
Why people chose this path;
When all seems lost;
Its over; so quick and fast.

I am so fortunate;
Yet I feel that I'm not;
Without you my love;
What have I got?

Come to me; come to me;
The tracks are calling;
I feel myself slowly;
Falling . . . . falling.

I just don't know;
What is stopping me;
Perhaps it's all the people;
That would have to see.

I don't know if I can go on;
The emptiness is killing me;
Without you I'm nothing;
Why can't anyone see?

The pain that's inside me;
Slowly eating me away;
The loss of you is too much;
Yet everyone thinks I'm okay.

I've contemplated tablets;
I've even tied a noose;
Anything that will release me;
Release me and set me loose.

There's no reason to go on;
No reason to even care;
Yet with no other soul;
Am I willing this to share.

The nights are the hardest;
My days filled with work;
It's during these long nights;
That these thoughts most lurk.

Each day is a challenge;
I don't know if I can win;
In the eyes of God however;
Suicide would be a sin.

You believed in me;
When others couldn't;
Didn't want to;
Or simply, wouldn't.

You saw;
Saw in me;
Something special;
Something others couldn't see.

You held out your wings;
Took me by the hand;
Told me I could do anything;
Yes, yes you can.

You told me I was special;
Told me that you cared;
That you'd never hurt me;
Look at how I've faired.

You let go of me;
When you said you wouldn't;
Let me crash and fall;
This; you knew you shouldn't.

I hope you understand;
Your last words to me;
No! I just don't;
But I have to let you be.

Should I publish; should I not?
Will it hurt him? Will it not?
Will he know? Probably never;
What the heck; sign on the dot.

He made his choice by text;
That fateful October day;
To severe our relationship;
Without a word did he say.

He made a conscious choice;
Now I must make mine;
Should I consult with him?
I know where him to find.

Would he show me the same?
Courtesy and respect;
If he was in my position;
Knowing it may affect.

He told me I should publish;
On more than one occasion;
Why am I questioning, when?
We no longer have a liaison.

Two wrongs don't make a right;
Or so they say;
This could hurt him;
It just may.